BIG BILL

I0139760

A R Gurney

BROADWAY PLAY PUBLISHING INC
New York
www.broadwayplaypublishing.com
info@broadwayplaypublishing.com

BIG BILL
© Copyright 2004 by A R Gurney

Cover art by James McMullan
First printing: February 2004
I S B N: 978-0-88145-234-1

Book design: Marie Donovan
Word processing: Microsoft Word for Windows
Typographic controls: Xerox Ventura Publisher 2.0 P E
Typeface: Palatino
Printed and bound in the U S A

ORIGINAL PRODUCTION

BIG BILL was first produced at the Williamstown
Theater Festival (Michael Ritchie, Producer), opening
on 2 July 2003. The play subsequently transferred to the
Mitzi E Newhouse Theater at Lincoln Center (André
Bishop, Artistic Director; Bernard Gersten, Executive
Producer), opening on 22 February 2004. The cast and
creative contributors were:

WILLIAM TATEM TILDEN II . . . . . John Michael Higgins
UMPIRE, JUDGE *and others* . . . . David Cromwell
HERB, MADDOX *and others* . . . . .Stephen Rowe
MARY, SUZANNE *and others* . . . . Margaret Welch

in Williamstown:
ARTHUR, BALL BOYS *and others* . . . . Gideon Banner

in New York:
ARTHUR *and others* . . . . .Jeremiah Miller
STUDENT *and others* . . . . Alex Knold
PETE *and others* . . . . Michael Esper
JIMMY *and others* . . . . .Donal Thoms-Cappello

Director . . . . Mark Lamos
Set design . . . . .John Lee Beatty
Costumes . . . . Jess Goldstein
Lighting . . . . Rui Rita
Production stage manager . . . . Fred H Orner

in New York:
Sound . . . . .Scott Stauffer

CHARACTERS & SETTING

WILLIAM TATEM TILDEN, II, *otherwise known as Big Bill*
FIRST ACTOR, *to play various authority figures, such as a*
tennis official, a judge, and a drama critic
SECOND ACTOR, *to play* TILDEN's *brother, and other*
supportive types
ACTRESS, *to play all the women*
Two or more YOUNGER ACTORS, *to play ball boys, younger*
men, and assist with props, costume pieces, and the
movement of furniture.

A generalized playing area, primarily green, suggesting that
special color of forest green associated with older tennis
arenas, such as Wimbledon or Forest Hills. The main
elements of the set should invoke the underlying image of
tennis: an ivy-covered background, green canvas screening,
a "change-over area", consisting of a couple of wooden chairs
with a table between them, perhaps a bench, and upstage
center, a raised green umpire's chair with a tray-like
attachment on which the umpire keeps score. These elements
transform into various other spaces during the course of the
play, but the subliminal sense of a tennis game should prevail
throughout. The ground cover should convey the suggestion
of green grass.

Costumes: TILDEN *wears mostly a white V-necked cable-*
stitched tennis sweater, with maroon and blue stripes at the
neck and long white flannel trousers, sometimes adding a
rather ratty camel's hair overcoat or a loose tweed jacket.
The others wear basically what is necessary to establish their

characters. The ball boys wear sneakers, shorts and matching polo shirts.

Music: Occasionally, popular songs from a particular era might be used to set the tone of a scene and help anchor the period, but they are not necessary every time.

The play should run about ninety minutes and has no intermission.

NOTE

This play is indebted to *Big Bill Tilden* by Frank Deford, *Tilden and Tennis in the Twenties* by Arthur Voss, and other material, including writings by Tilden himself.

for Mark Lamos with great appreciation

(Before rise: a popular song from the Twenties, in a scratchy primitive recording.)

(At rise: the music modulates into the sounds of a tennis match: first, the thwack of rackets hitting the ball, then the swelling cheers and applause of a large and appreciative crowd as the lights come up on the stage.)

(In the "stands" are three enthusiastic fans, watching a tennis game: a MAN, a YOUNGER MAN, and a WOMAN. They wear summer clothes, with hats or sunshades, suggesting the Twenties. They cheer, applaud, and move their heads in unison as the sounds of the game continue.)

(From the elevated umpire's chair, the UMPIRE calls out the score through a hand-held megaphone, and writes it down on a wooden clipboard. He wears a light, striped blazer and an old-fashioned tennis visor.)

(On either side of the UMPIRE's chair, two BALL BOYS crouch at the ready. They wear sneakers, socks, shorts, and polo shirts.)

(The sound of a serve)

UMPIRE: *(Pronouncing his words carefully)* Fifteen-love.

(A BALL BOY dashes off as if to retrieve the ball.)

(Sound of another serve. The people in the stands applaud. It is obviously an ace.)

UMPIRE: Thirty-love.

MAN: *(To WOMAN)* That's what Tilden calls his American Twist.

WOMAN: It's beautiful!

YOUNG MAN: It's unreturnable!

(Another serve, more applause, another point)

(A second BALL BOY runs off.)

UMPIRE: Forty-love.

(A sense of restlessness)

YOUNG MAN: Now what?

MAN: Tilden is stopping play.

UMPIRE: *(On megaphone)* Quiet, please. Mr Tilden wishes to speak to the chair.

(TILDEN hurries on, carrying a wooden racket. He wears long white flannel trousers and a white, long-sleeved shirt. A BALL BOY follows him, handing him a towel.)

TILDEN: *(To group in stands)* Please excuse the interruption, my friends. But some things cannot stand. *(To UMPIRE)* I can't accept that last point, Fred. My serve was out.

UMPIRE: The linesman didn't think so, Bill.

TILDEN: The linesman is wrong.

UMPIRE: *(Through megaphone)* Attention, linesman: do you wish to change your call? *(Listens; then to TILDEN)* Linesman stands by his call, Bill.

TILDEN: Over-rule him, Fred. My serve was half an inch out.

UMPIRE: I will not over-rule him.

TILDEN: The man has made shaky calls all afternoon! I was looking right down the line!

UMPIRE: Bill...

(They confer privately.)

WOMAN: *(To OLDER MAN)* Does Tilden do this a lot?

MAN: When he thinks the call is wrong.

YOUNG MAN: Why?

MAN: Because he's the ultimate sportsman.

YOUNG MAN: *(Impatiently calling out)* Play ball, Bill!

TILDEN: *(To* YOUNG MAN*)* Did you say something, young man?

YOUNG MAN: *(Cowed)* I just wanted you to go on playing.

TILDEN: Let me tell you something, my young friend. A bad call makes for a bad game. And in a bad game, everybody loses—you spectators most of all.

WOMAN: *(To* MAN*)* You'd think they'd simply play the point over.

MAN: They don't do that in tournament tennis.

TILDEN: *(Overhearing)* We don't do that in life, either, dear lady!

UMPIRE: *(Exasperated)* What *do* we do then, Bill?

TILDEN: We get rid of bad linesmen.

UMPIRE: Sorry, Bill! No soap.

TILDEN: Then there's only one solution. *(He storms off.)*

UMPIRE: *(Calling out formally)* The score is, and remains, forty-love. Mr Tilden leads, five games to two, in the third set...Mr Tilden will serve.

(Sound of a serve)

YOUNG MAN: What a dinky serve.

(Sounds of a point being played)

WOMAN: He's hardly bothering.

MAN: He's giving away the point.

(Weak applause)

UMPIRE: Forty-fifteen.

MAN: See?

YOUNG MAN: Anyway he was three points ahead.

MAN: He does that even when he's behind, if he dislikes a call.

WOMAN: How strange.

MAN: He's a strange guy. Now comes the *coup de grace.*

(Sound of another serve)

YOUNG MAN: Holy smokes!

MAN: That was his cannon-ball serve!

WOMAN: I could hardly see the ball!

YOUNG MAN: Neither could his opponent.

UMPIRE: Game, set, and match to Mr Tilden.

(The group applauds and stands up. TILDEN comes on again, perfunctorily shakes the UMPIRE's hand.)

TILDEN: Thank you, Fred.

UMPIRE: You're a pain in the neck, Bill.

TILDEN: *(Toweling himself off)* Can't win on a bad call. Would have felt humiliated.

UMPIRE: *(Stepping down from his elevated seat)* So you humiliated the linesman instead. *(He goes.)*

TILDEN: *(Calling after him)* Next time he'll stay awake! *(To group in stands)* Tennis can be a beautiful game, my friends, when it's played by sportsmen and gentlemen.

WOMAN: You make it beautiful, Mr Tilden!

TILDEN: *(Saluting her with his racket)* Thank you, dear lady! I certainly try!

(He gathers up his other rackets, and goes off, followed by his BALL BOY.)

(A popular song from Sixties is heard as the WOMAN *picks up a stack of books, puts on reading glasses and a matronly sweater. She becomes a* LIBRARIAN *at the University of Pennsylvania. She crosses to the change-over table and begins to stamp the books.* YOUNG ACTOR *approaches her, now as a* STUDENT, *wearing a jacket and carrying a notebook or two.)*

STUDENT: Excuse me. Could you tell me—

LIBRARIAN: Ssshh! We are in a library, young man.

STUDENT: *(Lowering his voice)* I just want to know if you found those books?

LIBRARIAN: What books?

STUDENT: The books on Tilden? Big Bill Tilden?
The tennis player? I'm writing a paper on him.

LIBRARIAN: Oh yes.

STUDENT: The card catalogue lists lots of books, by him and about him. But they're not in the stacks. You were going to check on them, remember?

LIBRARIAN: Oh yes.

STUDENT: So. Do you have them?

LIBRARIAN: *(Stamping her books vigorously)* I do not.

STUDENT: But Tilden *went* here! He graduated from Penn!

LIBRARIAN: I believe there's some question about that.

STUDENT: I just don't get it! We're talking about a major figure in sports. My grandfather used to tell me about him all the time! *(Reading from his notebook)* Big Bill Tilden. First American ever to win Wimbledon, and later, the oldest player ever to win there! And you want to know what he won over here?

LIBRARIAN: Ssshh.

STUDENT: And listen to what I found in the World Almanac. *(Reads more)* In 1949, the Associated Press voted Tilden the greatest American athlete in his field, for the first half of the Twentieth Century. He got ten times as many votes as his nearest competitor. Isn't that amazing? More than Bobby Jones. Or Red Grange. Or even Babe Ruth. And you're saying we don't have any books on him?

LIBRARIAN: *(Gathering up her books, starting off)* If you must know, some time in the Fifties, the Library Committee voted to remove the Tilden material.

STUDENT: Why?

LIBRARIAN: I don't know.

STUDENT: Are his books in the cellar somewhere?

LIBRARIAN: I don't know that either.

STUDENT: How do I check?

LIBRARIAN: Perhaps if you petitioned the Library Committee.

STUDENT: But my paper's due in two weeks!

LIBRARIAN: *(Starting out)* Perhaps you should write about something more important than tennis.

STUDENT: *(Following her)* But Tilden *made* it important! That's why I want to write about him!

LIBRARIAN: Ssshh!

(They exit as the UMPIRE *comes on, now in* JUDGE's *robes. He mounts the* UMPIRE's *chair and bangs his gavel.)*

JUDGE: Next case... *(Reads from a document)* William Tatem Tilden, the Second.

*(*TILDEN *appears, now wearing a ratty old camel's hair overcoat over his tennis clothes, along with an elegant white scarf at his neck.)*

JUDGE: The tennis player?

TILDEN: Yes, sir.

JUDGE: You reside here in Los Angeles, Mr Tilden?

TILDEN: I do now, sir.

JUDGE: *(Glancing at documents)* Born in Philadelphia?

TILDEN: Yes sir.

JUDGE: City of Brotherly Love.

TILDEN: So they say.

JUDGE: Do you have an occupation, Mr Tilden?

TILDEN: Tennis, sir.

JUDGE: Other than tennis.

TILDEN: Tennis is it, sir.

JUDGE: But your source of income is...?

TILDEN: Tennis, sir. I teach at several of the local clubs and occasionally play in professional tournaments.

JUDGE: Are you aware of the charges against you, Mr Tilden?

TILDEN: I find all this somewhat embarrassing.

JUDGE: Answer my question, please.

TILDEN: The answer is yes.

JUDGE: Would you be willing to sign a document attesting to these events?

(A YOUNG ACTOR *wearing a* POLICEMAN's *hat and shirt presents* TILDEN *with a clipboard and pen.)*

TILDEN: I'm sorry. I don't have my glasses.

JUDGE: The officer will read it aloud.

TILDEN: *(Quickly)* No, don't! Please! I don't need to hear it! *(Takes the pen, signs quickly)*

JUDGE: You're not obligated to sign, Mr Tilden.

TILDEN: Ah, but apparently I reached across the net, didn't I?

JUDGE: Reached across...?

TILDEN: The net. If you do that in tennis, you lose the point.

JUDGE: Then yes, you definitely reached across the net, Mr Tilden.

TILDEN: *(Handing the document back)* I have always had a great regard for the law. *(To* POLICEMAN*)* And I have always respected law enforcement officers.

*(*POLICEMAN *goes off.)*

JUDGE: I follow sports a little, Mr Tilden.

TILDEN: Do you?

JUDGE: Enough to know you were once a great tennis player.

TILDEN: Once? Still am, your honor. I took a set off Jack Kramer at a charity event just last week.

JUDGE: Jack Kramer.

TILDEN: He's the best we have these days. And half my age.

JUDGE: I hear you have friends among the stars.

TILDEN: Oh yes. Clark Gable. Douglas Fairbanks. Charlie Chaplin.

JUDGE: I read somewhere that you play tennis with them.

TILDEN: When they ask me, sir.

JUDGE: Any of them any good?

TILDEN: They're better when they play with me.

JUDGE: And you say you teach, too.

TILDEN: Oh yes. Joseph Cotten. Katharine Hepburn. Even Garbo has taken a lesson or two.

JUDGE: I'm releasing you on your own recognizance, Mr Tilden.

TILDEN: Thank you, sir.

JUDGE: And may I strongly suggest that you modify your game.

TILDEN: I definitely will, sir. *(He starts out.)*

JUDGE: But you're not off the hook, Mr Tilden.

TILDEN: Sir?

JUDGE: May I suggest that you get yourself a lawyer. I intend to indict you, Mr Tilden. I am sending your case to trial. *(He leaves.)*

*(*TILDEN *stands shocked, as* SECOND ACTOR *comes on as* HERB, TILDEN's *older brother.)*

HERB: *(Calling)* June! ...Come over here, Junie! Let's have a brotherly chat.

*(*TILDEN *tosses aside his overcoat, becoming a young man as he joins his brother at the table.)*

TILDEN: I wish you wouldn't call me that, Herb.

HERB: Call you what?

TILDEN: Junie... It's a girl's name.

HERB: It's just a nickname for Junior.

TILDEN: Mother started it, and I hate it. Now she's gone, it's time to cut it out.

HERB: Shall we settle for Junior then?

TILDEN: No!

HERB: Why not? It reminds people that you're the son of one of the most distinguished businessmen in Philadelphia. *(He signals for a* WAITER.*)*

TILDEN: It reminds people to tease me, every chance they get. One of these days I'm going to legally change my name to William Tatum Tilden the *Second*. Then no one can call me sissy Junie ever again.

(One of the YOUNG ACTORS *comes on, in a white jacket, as a* WAITER.*)*

HERB: Two beers, please.

TILDEN: *One* beer, and one birch beer for me.

HERB: Still won't drink?

TILDEN: Alcohol makes me say and do things I'm sorry for later.

(The WAITER *starts off.* TILDEN *glances after him)*

HERB: O K, um, Bill. Is Bill O K?

TILDEN: Bill's fine.

HERB: Dad asked me to have a talk with you....

*(*TILDEN *is distracted by watching the* WAITER *go.)*

TILDEN: Sorry... Why doesn't Dad ask me himself? He's just in the game room, shooting billiards, last time I looked.

HERB: He finds you hard to talk to.

TILDEN: *(Imitating father)* "Can't speak to the boy. Never could."

HERB: *(Laughing)* You've got his number, all right.

TILDEN: "Buy him a drink... Put it on my tab... Light a fire under the boy."

HERB: You're a good actor.

TILDEN: I've had to be.

HERB: Dad thinks it's time you decided what you want to do.

TILDEN: Do?

HERB: With your *life*, Junie. Now that mother's gone.

TILDEN: *(Imitating his father again)* "Roll up your sleeves, lad... Put your shoulder to the wheel..."

HERB: He's cooked up a job for you.

TILDEN: Last week he suggested the antique business.

HERB: Why did you say no? You like antiques.

TILDEN: I don't like the connotations.

HERB: What connotations?

TILDEN: Sissy stuff. Escorting Mrs Shumaker to the flower show. Being the extra man at a dinner party. No thanks. What's this week's proposal?

HERB: Teaching English at Germantown Academy.

TILDEN: I should have guessed.

HERB: He's already spoken to the Headmaster. The salary's not great, but Dad will continue your allowance. And it's close to home.

TILDEN: So he can keep an eye on me?

HERB: So he can see more of you. He loves you, Bill.

TILDEN: I know, I know. In his way.

HERB: Take the teaching job. You like books and you're good with kids. It's an ideal job for a bachelor.

TILDEN: Father used that word? Bachelor?

HERB: He might have, yes.

TILDEN: What if I get married?

(WAITER comes out.)

WAITER: *(To* HERB*)* Anything else, sir?

HERB: No thanks. We're fine.

*(*WAITER *goes off.* TILDEN *watches him again.)*

HERB: Thinking of getting married, Bill?

TILDEN: *(Snapping out of it)* Not at the moment, no.

HERB: Nothing wrong with being a bachelor.

TILDEN: Nothing wrong at all. Especially if you tuck him away in an antique store or a private school.

HERB: Come on, Bill.

TILDEN: Yes, well tell Dad I've got other plans.

HERB: Such as what.

TILDEN: Tennis.

HERB: Tennis?

TILDEN: Put a racket in my hand, and I'm transformed, Herb! I feel strong, I feel clean. I feel like a true man!

HERB: You can't make a life out of tennis, for God's sake.

TILDEN: Maybe I can.

HERB: You didn't even make the varsity at Penn.

TILDEN: That's because my mind was clouded, with Mother sick and all. I'm stronger now, and I'm taking the game seriously.

HERB: Which reminds me. The neighbors called about your banging the ball against the garage door all day long.

TILDEN: Practice makes perfect, Herb. I beat Sedgewick this morning.

HERB: You beat the Club pro?

TILDEN: Six-two, six-three. And now I want to enter some major tournaments. Dad can stake me to tennis.

I'm working on a whole new arsenal of strokes. And a whole new theory on how to use them. . *(He gets up to go.)*

HERB: Where are you going?

TILDEN: To find an empty squash court. I've got a match this afternoon. I need to fix a kink in my backhand.

HERB: So what do I tell Dad?

TILDEN: Tell him to call me Bill.

HERB: He'll say ...

TILDEN: *(Imitating his father again; HERB joins him.)* "The city of Philadelphia isn't big enough for two Bill Tildens."

HERB: That's exactly what he'll say.

TILDEN: Then tell him this, Herb: he can be Old Bill, the successful businessman. And I'll be Young Bill— no, *Big* Bill—champion tennis player and father of a winning game!

(They exit, either way as we hear a soprano's voice singing an aria from French opera.)

(ACTRESS enters, elegantly dressed. Now she is MARY GARDEN, the opera singer.)

MARY: *(Calling off)* You there! Ballboy!

(YOUNG ACTOR comes on as a BALL BOY.)

BALL BOY: Ma'am?

MARY: Where do I find the celebrated tennis player, Mr Bill Tilden?

BALL BOY: He's in the locker room, Ma'am.

MARY: Is he? I waited endlessly by the door, like some stage-door Johnny. The others came out, but not Mr Tilden.

BALL BOY: Mr Tilden always takes his shower last, Ma'am. He likes his privacy.

MARY: Then please go knock on the door, and tell him his public awaits him.

BALL BOY: Who shall I say you are, ma'am?

MARY: Say that I am an avid fan. And add that I am a famous opera star by the name of Mary Garden.

BALL BOY: *(Impressed)* Yes, ma'am! *(He goes.)*

(MARY arranges herself dramatically, as TILDEN hurries on, still in his tennis clothes)

TILDEN: Miss Garden! I'm honored.

(They shake hands.)

MARY: As am I, Mr Tilden. Have I interrupted your shower?

TILDEN: That can wait.

MARY: Good, because I have something to say. You are exceptional, sir. I came here today to see what all the fuss was about and you fulfilled every expectation.

TILDEN: I didn't know you were a tennis fan.

MARY: I am a fan of excellence wherever it occurs. I am a fan of the fiction of Mr F Scott Fitzgerald. I am a fan of the paintings of Monsieur Henri Matisse. And just now I have become a devoted fan of Mr William Tilden, the tennis player.

TILDEN: You're putting me in exalted company.

MARY: Because you are an artist, dear sir. I sensed it the minute you walked out on the court and saluted the audience with your tennis racket.

TILDEN: I do that sometimes. *(He might do it now)*

MARY: I do the same sort of thing. Once, in *La Traviata,* I tossed camellias into the front row.

TILDEN: I saw you do that in London.

MARY: What? An athlete who goes to the opera?

TILDEN: Whenever I can.

MARY: Well, the audiences are the same in either case, aren't they? Enthusiasts all, and eager to let us know it.

TILDEN: If you guide them.

MARY: Exactly! Which you do, dear sir! I adored the way you kept calming us down or stirring us up. You were conducting us—like Maestro Toscanini!

TILDEN: The sportswriters say I'm shameless.

MARY: Ah,, but all artists have their critics. Heaven knows I have mine. Critics are like flies—we must swat them away. But now a serious question: did you lose that second set on purpose?

TILDEN: Me? Lose? On purpose? Never!

MARY: Except that you did, didn't you?

TILDEN: *(Slyly)* If I did, it was to make the third set more exciting.

MARY: Which it was, which it was! Oh, Mr Tilden, you managed to give a shape to the entire afternoon.

TILDEN: Do you like to mix up your strokes?

MARY: Always! I like to follow a strong crescendo with a light glissando. And you?

TILDEN: Me, I have developed what I call my own sweet game. I vary my cannonball serve with an American twist. And I've developed three kinds of forehands, namely a chop, a top-spin and a flat, standard drive.

I've built up a whole repertory of shots, for every situation.

MARY: That's it! That's it! And I adore the way you compliment your opponent.

TILDEN: When he's hit a good shot, I let him know it.

MARY: You shouted, "Peach!" at the top of your lungs. "That shot of yours was a peach!" Of course I did the same thing at La Scala. When Martinelli hit his high C, I shouted "bravo" right there on stage, so we could all applaud.

TILDEN: And I'll bet you got a big hand at the curtain call.

MARY: Bigger than Martinelli's, actually.

TILDEN: Sometimes they don't applaud at all.

MARY: Oh yes, the fools. How little they know, in the end.

TILDEN: All the more reason to teach them! Sometimes, I simply stop the game and put my hands on my hips like this... (*He demonstrates.*) ...and wait till they applaud.

MARY: I'll try that next week in Chicago.

TILDEN: I'll be there when you do.

MARY: You'll find two tickets at the box office under your name.

TILDEN: One is enough.

MARY: What? Only one? For a great athlete like yourself? Surely you have some lovely little bit of fluff who rushes into your arms after a game.

TILDEN: Not really. No.

MARY: I see. Because you're an artist, sir. And artists are all ultimately alone. (*Starts out*) Now after the opera, I want you to stop by my dressing room. So we can become better friends.

TILDEN: I will.

MARY: Meanwhile, *adio!* Oh, I knew you'd be a kindred spirit! I could sniff you out immediately! Which reminds me. Perhaps now's the time to take that shower.

(She goes. TILDEN *stands looking after her as the* FIRST ACTOR *comes on as* STUART, *President of the Germantown Cricket Club. He holds a glass in his hand and is mildly and happily inebriated.)*

STUART: *(To audience)* Members and guests of the Germantown Cricket Club: it is my great pleasure to present to you our native son: Mr William Tatem Tilden, the Second , tennis-player extraordinaire...

*(*TILDEN *crosses to him, shakes hands.)*

STUART: Welcome home, Bill.

TILDEN: Home?

STUART: We all hope you still consider Philadelphia your home.

TILDEN: Home is where you hang your hat. And I don't wear hats.

STUART: Ah, but you grew up here.

TILDEN: "Grew up" here? I suppose. I was born here. Went to school here. Buried my entire family here. Mother, father, brother—laid them to rest here, one after one, all within a period of less than four years. So yes, I grew up fast.

STUART: I'm sorry, Bill.

TILDEN: So am I. Very. But do you know where I really grew up? On the tennis court.

STUART: You sure have. *(To audience)* This man is now known throughout the tennis world as Big Bill Tilden.

TILDEN: The sportswriters call me that. I'm not that tall, but they say I seem big on the court.

STUART: Remember, gang? When we used to call him little Junie Tilden?

TILDEN: *(Irritated)* I thought I was asked to talk about tennis.

STUART: Right. Your serve, Bill. *(He withdraws.)*

TILDEN: *(To audience)* Let's start with the golden rule of all athletics. Always play to win. Never play just not to lose. Every match is a battle, within and without. Cultivate a killer instinct in your soul, but be a sportsman to the world. Be murderous but courteous. The tough thing is to reconcile the two. *(Indicates his sweater)* Which leads us to clothes. In tennis, we wear white. It's cooler, of course. And more attractive—by that I mean it's less likely to display unsightly patches of perspiration. And of course white makes the players more visible from the higher seats in the newer stadiums. And we always play better when we're watched, don't we? But there's yet another reason for whiteness. You'll notice that in the Bible the angels of the Lord always appear in white raiment. Why? Because white is pure, white is innocent. And tennis is an innocent game. That's why I don't approve of shorts. There's a young player in Grosse Point—good serve, exceptional net game—who wears shorts, at least in practice. I find it distracting. It says in the Bible, "take no delight in a man's legs." Nor a woman's, either, I hasten to add. Men should wear long white trousers. Women, white stockings. The whiteness is what we want, not naked flesh. I hope we're all agreed on that. *(Taking up his racket)* Now for the tool of our trade. Our Excalibur! *(Displays it)* Consider the stringing. All

rackets should be strung with gut, preferably taken
from the intestines of a young lamb ... *(Strums his
racket like a guitar)* Listen to that sound. *(Sings)*
"Ain't she sweet... Don't she knock you off your feet?"
...Nowadays there is talk of shifting to manufactured
fibers, but I much prefer real gut. It's organic, it has
texture, it puts more spin on the ball. Keep it natural,
say I. Natural strings in a wooden racket. Lately, in
my wanderings, I've noticed that some players are
beginning to wrap their grips with leather. They say
their hands are less likely to slip. Not me. I like to sense
the grain of the wood. It tells me where I am. *(Holds it
up)* My rod and my staff! It comforts me. *(Sits)* Let's
now talk about feet. *(Removes his shoes)* Sneakers are
important, of course. But not as important as shoe
salesmen would have us believe. Many times during
a match, I play in bare feet. *(Wiggles his toes)* Why?
Because you can feel the give of the grass. Or if it's clay,
you can sense its density. You can dig in your heels or
use your toes for purchase. *(Moves around)* See? I'm
grounded. I'm connected.... Ah, but I need a guinea
pig... *(Points off)* You there.

(A YOUNG ACTOR *comes on hesitantly; call him* TONY.*)*

TONY: Me?

TILDEN: Step out here, please. We'll demonstrate the
basic stance in tennis.

TONY: *(Proudly, grinning at audience)* O K!

TILDEN: '*(Handing him the racket)* Take the racket.
That's it. Shake hands with it, as if it were the best
friend you'll ever have - which it may turn out to be.
(Demonstrates) Good. Firmly, but not too tight. Give
your fingers some play. Yes. Good. *(Stands behind him)*
Make sure that this V...this V for Victory... *(Reaching
around, touching the* TONY's *hand)* between your thumb
and forefinger, make sure it settles on the top of the

handle. Yes. Now this is what we call the continental
grip. *(The lesson becomes more intimate as* TILDEN *stands
behind his pupil, with his hand on top of the pupil's hand,
guiding his swing.)* Yes, all right now, stand sideways,
like this, with your left leg forward. *(Moves the* TONY*'s
leg forward)* Yes. Now the ball is coming, so get your
arm back in plenty of time, yes...good...now, now step
forward and meet the ball out in front of you...there!
Yes! And follow through all the way! *(They end in a
strongly intimate position.)* There. That's your basic
forehand drive. Build on that, and all will be well.
(He steps away.)

*(*TONY *is obviously uncomfortable.)*

TILDEN: Thank you, my young friend.

(As TONY *exits,* TILDEN *pats his rear with his racket,
then begins to move gracefully around the stage,
demonstrating the various strokes of tennis.)*

TILDEN: Because footwork is everything, people.
You see? It's like a dance. ...The serve... Pow! ...the
forehand... Pow! ...the backhand...the rush to net... Pow,
pow, pow! You see? Look at me. I'm a dancer, really...
I'm Nijinksy, I'm Valentino, I'm—who's that young
dancer who performs on Broadway with his sister?
I'm Fred Astaire! *(He uses his racket as a cane.)* "Puttin'
on the Ritz"... And I'm not being facetious here, folks.
The player owes the gallery as much as the actor owes
his audience... *(He calms down.)* But I've come to learn
that the attention span of American audiences is
somewhat limited, so that's enough lecture for tonight.

*(He bows, salutes the audience with his racket. He sits down,
puts his shoes back on, as* STUART *returns.)*

STUART: *(To audience)* How about that, gang? How
about that? *(Shaking* TILDEN*'s hand)* Your father always
said you'd make a good teacher, Bill.

TILDEN: *(Imitating his father)* "If the shoe fits, put it on..." *(He puts on his shoes.)*

STUART: He was stalwart member of the community, your father.

TILDEN: Stalwart—and broke, when he died. Did you know that?

STUART: We heard that. I'm sorry.

TILDEN: You might say he used up his strokes in the first two sets of his match.

STUART: *(Holding out a check)* I hope this helps. It's not much, but it's our usual honorarium.

TILDEN: *(Not taking the check)* I can't accept money, Stuart.

STUART: We pay all our lecturers.

TILDEN: You don't pay me. I'd lose my amateur standing. It would keep me out of all the big tournaments, and the Davis Cup besides.

STUART: I doubt very much that the United States Lawn Tennis Association would object to this small token.

TILDEN: They might not, but I do. *(Putting his racket in a press)* I take my status seriously, sir. I am an "amateur." *Amo, amas,* amateur. From the Latin, meaning "to love." I love the game. I married it for love. I am loyal to it for love. If I accepted money for playing tennis, I'd feel like a whore.

(He goes; STUART looks after him. TONY comes back on.)

TONY: What's the problem?

STUART: He wouldn't accept our check.

TONY: So what? We paid his transportation. We put him up. We gave him dinner.

STUART: True enough...

(They start out together.)

STUART: Did you like your lesson?

TONY: I guess.

STUART: You guess? A major player taught you how to stroke the ball!

TONY: I'd like it better if he stayed on his side of the net.

(They go off, as SECOND ACTOR *comes on as* RICHARD MADDOX, *a Los Angeles lawyer, reading a legal document. He sits at the change-over table as if it were his desk. After a moment,* TILDEN *comes in, now wearing his ratty camel's hair coat.)*

MADDOX: *(Looking up)* I've decided to take your case, Mr Tilden.

TILDEN: Good. Fine. Absolutely delighted.

MADDOX: Though I'm not sure why. I have to tell you I'm uncomfortable with what you're accused of.

TILDEN: Would it help if I said so am I?

MADDOX: I'm serious. This business goes very much against my grain. What's worse, it won't be easy. The toughest cases are those where a dog or a child is the victim.

TILDEN: I'm very fond of dogs.

MADDOX: *(Indicating folder)* And of children, apparently.

TILDEN: This was no child.

MADDOX: A young man, then.

TILDEN: A very old young man. He'd been around, let me tell you.

MADDOX: So have you, Mr Tilden. For... *(Checking folder)* ...fifty-three years.

TILDEN: Yes, but I like to think I've lived a sheltered life.

MADDOX: Sheltered is it? Well, maybe so. Maybe that's why.... *(Taking out a document)* ...you signed this incriminating statement.

TILDEN: Oh, well, that.

MADDOX: The judge tells me you didn't even bother to read it.

TILDEN: Ah, but we have to trust the umpire, don't we?

MADDOX: This is not a game, Mr Tilden! You're in deep trouble.

TILDEN: Am I? Seriously?

MADDOX: Deep, deep trouble. Surely you realize that. Has this sort of thing ever happened before?

TILDEN: Well now, let's review the bidding here.... *(Looks around)* I can be frank with my lawyer, can't I?

MADDOX: It usually helps.

TILDEN: Has this happened before. The answer is, yes and no.

MADDOX: Let's concern ourselves with the "yes".

TILDEN: All right then, yes—but rarely. And only recently. After I started to lose. When I was winning, I would never, ever.... But lately I have a tendency to lose...my grip.

MADDOX: That's a rather cavalier way of putting it.

TILDEN: Well these incidents are nuisances more than anything else.

MADDOX: Nuisances?

TILDEN: The English have ways of handling these things. They're especially good at sweeping them under the—

MADDOX: I'm not interested in the English, Mr Tilden.
I'm interested only in defending you as best I can.

TILDEN: Right. I understand.

MADDOX: Then listen to me, sir. You are indicted!
You could go to jail!

TILDEN: Oh now please.

MADDOX: They're looking for headlines here in L A!
Do you know who the Judge is?

TILDEN: I understand he's a gentleman named Scott.
I'm hoping he'll let me off scott-free.

MADDOX: Mr Tilden! Perhaps I'm old fashioned, but I
find none of this funny.

TILDEN: Oh but I'm serious when I'm funny. Read
my book, "The Art of Lawn Tennis." There I say that
a smile always wins points because it gives the
impression of confidence.

MADDOX: Judge A A Scott happens to be the son of Joe
Scott. And Joe Scott was the lawyer who nailed Chaplin
on that paternity suit.

TILDEN: Did Charlie telephone you? He's a good friend.
He sees me as a fellow artist.

MADDOX: He thinks you should leave the country.
Which is probably what he'll have to do himself.

TILDEN: Leave the country?

MADDOX: The war's just over, sir, and people are trying
to put the world back together. They're intolerant of
aberrant behavior. Now I don't know what you and
Chaplin have been up to out there on Summit Drive,
but apparently some people think you've been having
orgies between tennis matches.

TILDEN: Orgies?

MADDOX: Where he violates the girls and you violate the boys.

TILDEN: Oh for mercy's sake. And then we both dash off to join the Communist party?

MADDOX: That's what they probably think. (Laughing in spite of himself) Now you've got me laughing.

TILDEN: What did Voltaire say? "I laugh that I may not weep."

MADDOX: I don't know about Voltaire. I do know that I'm out of my element here. I probably should drop the case right now. (Pause) Except...

TILDEN: Except what?

MADDOX: Except I like you, Mr Tilden, Lord knows why.

TILDEN: Call me Bill. Everybody does.

MADDOX: Bill, then.

TILDEN: And I may call you what?

MADDOX: Richard.

TILDEN: Richard. I played some sensational matches with Richard Norris Williams. I remember a doubles match at Wimbledon—

MADDOX: Bill! Please! Try to focus

TILDEN: Okey doke. What do you advise me to do?

MADDOX: Plead not guilty and demand a jury trial.

TILDEN: Oh now really.

MADDOX: The case rests on the boy. And he's bad news. Divorced parents, in and out of schools. The kid is no sexual innocent, Bill.

TILDEN: We need no ghost from hell to tell us that!

MADDOX: According to his probation officer, he arranged the whole thing. Even told you where to pick him up.

TILDEN: He wanted me to take him to the movies.

MADDOX: So we'll say all that, and plead Not Guilty. A jury trial will automatically move us up to a different judge and prosecutor, where you'll have half a chance.

TILDEN: If I plead not guilty...

MADDOX: Right. If you go to trial at all. Which I doubt, because the parents of the kid won't want that kind of publicity. Money says they won't even let him testify. And without that, there's not much of a case, Bill. You'd probably get a suspended sentence.

TILDEN: But I signed that statement.

MADDOX: We'll say you were frightened and distraught.

TILDEN: Which I wasn't.

MADDOX: Which you were, goddammit! And still are! You just don't know it.

TILDEN: I don't think I can plead not guilty, Richard.

MADDOX: Why the hell not?

TILDEN: Because that would be cheating. How can I possibly deny this thing?

MADDOX: Don't take the stand.

TILDEN: So I'd have to sit there, listening to people talk about it? And read about it in the papers afterwards?

MADDOX: If it goes that far.

TILDEN: Oh God, this is so embarrassing.

MADDOX: You'll feel more embarrassed behind bars, Bill.

TILDEN: Oh now, do you really think they'd do that?
American tennis champion for nine straight years?
People from all over the world will be writing in to
support me! And I'm sure the Lawn Tennis Association
will ride to my rescue! No sirree, I can't plead not guilty.

MADDOX: Bill.

TILDEN: Oh look. I'm sure I'm due for some serious
finger-wagging. Maybe a little fine. Possibly even
a little psychiatric care. And that interests me, the
Freudian thing. All that subconscious stuff. I'd like
to know more about...why I do...what I do.

MADDOX: You are rejecting the advice of your lawyer,
then?

TILDEN: Have to, Richard. Pleading not guilty? That's
like trying to win a match on a bad call.

MADDOX: Let's at least go meet with the Judge. Talk
things through personally . Maybe he'll come around.

TILDEN: What? Go hat in hand to the umpire, begging
for a special deal? Can't do that, either, Richard. Not for
the life of me.

*(Lights fade on them as they exit. Tennis sounds .
The* UMPIRE *comes on, climbs into his chair.)*

UMPIRE: *(Calling out, with megaphone)* Game, set,
match to Mr Tilden.

(Sounds of crowd cheering and applause. Twenties music.
TILDEN *bounds back on, carrying a silver cup and a brace
of tennis rackets.)*

TILDEN: *(Shaking hands with the* UMPIRE*)* Good work,
Freddy! I had my doubts about one of your decisions,
but you were generally O K.

UMPIRE: May I speak to you privately, Bill?

TILDEN: Sure, What's up?

UMPIRE: *(Indicating table)* Let's go to the member's lounge.

TILDEN: Fine with me.

(They settle into the rest area chairs. A YOUNG ACTOR *comes on in another jacket as another* WAITER.*)*

UMPIRE: Drink, Bill?

TILDEN: You know I don't drink, Freddy.

UMPIRE: Never?

TILDEN: Did once. Got me into trouble.

UMPIRE: How?

TILDEN: That's for me to know and you never to find out.

UMPIRE: *(To* WAITER*)* Tom Collins, please.

TILDEN: *(To* WAITER*)* Water's fine.

WAITER: Yes, sir, Mr Tilden, sir.

*(*WAITER *goes off.* TILDEN *eyes him.)*

UMPIRE: Bill, I now have to put on my hat as President of the United States Lawn Tennis Association.

TILDEN: *(Saluting)* Aye, aye, sir.

UMPIRE: I've noticed your rackets. Those are the new Bancrofts, aren't they?

TILDEN: They are indeed. And the best model so far.

UMPIRE: I see they've put your name on them.

TILDEN: My name's on all the new models. *(Showing him the throat of the racket)* See? "Tilden-winner". Not bad, eh?

UMPIRE: Do they pay you, Bill? For the privilege of using your name?

TILDEN: Of course they don't pay me.

UMPIRE: Next thing, you'll be running around, wearing ads on your clothes.

TILDEN: That'll be the day.

UMPIRE: It's what money does, Bill. Now tennis is different from other sports. It's special, it's sacrosanct. And we want to keep it that way—totally uncorrupted by the marketplace.

TILDEN: I couldn't agree more.

(The WAITER *brings the drinks;* TILDEN *unconsciously checks him out.)*

UMPIRE: So please tell Bancroft to take those rackets off the shelves.

TILDEN: You tell them, Freddy. You seem to get a kick out of throwing your weight around.

UMPIRE: Oh and one other thing, Bill. Your magazine articles.

TILDEN: That's not advertising, Fred.

UMPIRE: No, but you've been writing up your own matches. And getting paid for it.

TILDEN: Freedom of speech, for God's sake!

UMPIRE: Say whatever you want. But not for money.

TILDEN: I've got to have an income, Freddy. I don't sit on a pile of stocks like the other players. This seems like a fair way to keep me solvent.

UMPIRE: We realize that. We might, therefore—I repeat might—allow you to publish paid articles about matches in which you don't actively participate.

TILDEN: That's big of you, sir. Seeing as how I actively participate in pretty much every match worth writing about. *(Starts out)*

UMPIRE: I hope we're still friends, Bill.

TILDEN: *(Dryly)* Oh sure. You bet.

UMPIRE: Because we're all very much looking forward to your defending your Wimbledon title next summer.

TILDEN: *(Stopping)* Oh you are, are you?

UMPIRE: Yes, and we're also hoping you'll go over early enough to play in the French Championships. We'll cover your travel expenses, of course.

TILDEN: The usual thousand dollars? Out of that enormous sum, I am supposed to pay my boat fare over and back, live three weeks in Paris and four in London.

UMPIRE: You'll stay at private residences, Bill, as all the players do. And your hosts will provide most of your meals.

TILDEN: Sorry, Fred. Think I'll stay home and write articles about events I'm not actively participating in. *(Starts out again)*

UMPIRE: Bill.

(TILDEN stops.)

UMPIRE: How much do you want?

TILDEN: First-class passage over and back.

UMPIRE: Bill...

TILDEN: The Ritz in Paris, the Savoy in London. Suites at both places.

UMPIRE: Bill!

TILDEN: And on the train between, my own compartment.

UMPIRE: Bill, this is silly. You like to live a Spartan life.

TILDEN: I've had to, Fred. Since my father died. But since you gentlemen are making all this dough these days—on me, I might add, on *me!*—maybe you should share the wealth.

UMPIRE: You're not an Indian rajah, Bill.

TILDEN: No, Freddie, I am not. But I'm a star. The first ever in this sport, if not in any other. And it's high time I looked the part.

(*He goes as the* UMPIRE *climbs into his chair*)

(*MUSIC: the Marseillaise*)

(WOMAN *enters wearing a bright pink headband and an elegant cardigan sweater. She carries a tennis racket. She is* SUZANNE LENGLEN, *the French Champion.*)

SUZANNE: (*To* UMPIRE; *French accent*) You wanted to speak to me, Monsieur.

UMPIRE: I've been asked to give you this note, Mademoiselle. (*Hands her a small blue envelope*)

SUZANNE: (*Looking at it*) Pour moi? Un billet-doux?

UMPIRE: You could look at it that way.

SUZANNE: (*Reading*) This is an invitation. To play tennis. From... (*Holding it out to the* UMPIRE) I cannot read this bad writing.

UMPIRE: William Tatum Tilden, the Second.

SUZANNE: Ah, but of course. "Beeg Beel." He's always making the challenges. Once he even sent a telegram. Is he here?

UMPIRE: Practicing for the French championships. Shall I tell him you'll play?

SUZANNE: *Ah non.* (*Crumbles up the note, tosses it aside*) *Jamais..*

UMPIRE: It would be an interesting match.

SUZANNE: Interesting, perhaps. Important, not at all. *Pardonnez-moi, Monsieur.* Now I must resume my regime. *(She proceeds to skip rope or do other sorts of elegant exercises.)*

(SECOND ACTOR comes on as an American tourist. He has a camera slung around his neck. He watches SUZANNE for a moment, then approaches the UMPIRE.)

TOURIST: Hey, who's the dame?

UMPIRE: That happens to be Suzanne Lenglen, the French champion.

TOURIST: She thinks she's the cat's ass, don't she?

UMPIRE: She's a major figure in tennis. She's taken the game to a higher level.

(They watch her exercise.)

UMPIRE: You might be interested to know that the English built Wimbledon for her. Last year, she played in front of ten thousand people, including the King and Queen.

TOURIST: What makes her such a hot ticket?

UMPIRE: Accuracy. They say that when she was young, her father would place a handkerchief at various spots on the court, and give her a five-franc piece every time she hit it with the ball

TOURIST: Money talks, huh?

UMPIRE: It does in France.

TOURIST: Does she ever play guys?

UMPIRE: All the time. And beats them, too.

TOURIST: Has she ever played Tilden?

UMPIRE: She keeps refusing, thank God. If she beat him, it would upset the whole international ranking.

TOURIST: I gotta get her picture. *(Going to her)* Pardon me, Mademoiselle...?

SUZANNE: Approach me.

TOURIST: May I take your photograph with our gang from Pittsburgh?

SUZANNE: Pittsburgh? I believe I am to play there on my tour of America. *D'accord.* A photograph is permissible.

TOURIST: *(Indicating off)* We're over by the Pavillion, eating crock mon-sieurs.

SUZANNE: *Tres bien. Allons-y.*

(They go off, SUZANNE *correcting his pronunciation, as* TILDEN *comes on with* PETE, *a ballboy.)*

TILDEN: *(To* UMPIRE, *as he watches them go)* Well?

UMPIRE: No soap.

TILDEN: Rats! I'd love to beat the pants off that woman.

UMPIRE: Why?

TILDEN: She gets my goat.

UMPIRE: Why don't you like women, Bill?

TILDEN: Women? I'm extremely fond of women. Some of my best friends are women. Mary Garden, the opera singer. Peggy Wood, the actress. I adore women.

UMPIRE: You won't even give them lessons.

TILDEN: That's because the chemistry isn't there. The magnetism. It just doesn't happen with women. Right, Pete?

PETE: Right

TILDEN: *(To* UMPIRE*)* Meet Pete. He's touring Europe with his parents before entering Yale.

PETE: *(To* UMPIRE*)* My Dad played with Bill in
Philadelphia.

TILDEN: I've been teaching Pete how to beat him.
(To PETE*)* Tell me, Pete. Does your mother still play?

PETE: She gave it up.

TILDEN: Why?

PETE: She says it makes her too nervous.

TILDEN: *(To* UMPIRE*)* You see, Freddy? The game
is different with women. Bridge, yes. Tennis no.
Women just...muddy the waters. Right, Pete?

PETE: Right.

UMPIRE: *(Looking off)* Here comes Mademoiselle Lenglen.

PETE: I'll bet you could beat her, Bill.

TILDEN: Hey, Freddy, how about this? What if I go rally
with Pete here over on court six. And play badly.

PETE: Play badly?

TILDEN: On purpose. So she'll rise to the bait.
(To UMPIRE*)* Get her to take a look, Freddie.

UMPIRE: I'm not going to serve as some pimp for—.

TILDEN: For tennis, Freddie! For tennis! It will clear
the air! Right, Pete?

PETE: Right, Bill! Let's do it.

*(*TILDEN *and* PETE *go.)*

(A moment. SUZANNE *returns.)*

SUZANNE: Was that Monsieur Beeg Beel?

UMPIRE: I believe it was.

SUZANNE: I hope the poor man finds a game.

UMPIRE: *(Looking)* He's got one already. With that boy.
Down on court six.

SUZANNE: I suppose I must take a little look. *(Watching)* He's not very good, is he? He lacks...consistency, *ne'est-ce pas?*

UMPIRE: He has his ups and downs.

SUZANNE: Today one might say he is down. *(Returning to her exercises)* Ah no. To play Tilden? It wouldn't work. One does not put meat loaf and pate de foie gras together on the same plate.

UMPIRE: It might provide good publicity for your tour.

SUZANNE: *Ah oui? (Watches again)* I might ask him simply to hit a ball or two. After all, I need practice. And obviously, so does he.

(She goes off. UMPIRE *watches. After a moment,* PETE *hurries back on.)*

PETE: *(To* UMPIRE*)* She's going for it.

UMPIRE: Is she?

PETE: Sure. Look. They're hitting. When I get to New Haven, I'm going to tell everybody that I helped Big Bill Tilden set a trap for Suzanne Lenglen!

UMPIRE: *(Dryly)* That should get you into Skull and Bones.

PETE: *(Looking off)* Don't you want to watch the proceedings?

UMPIRE: I can see from here.

PETE: *(Looking)* See? He's pretending he's totally off his game. That's why he's hitting those bloopers. *(Watches some more)* Now she's walking off the court ...

UMPIRE: Maybe she's had enough.

PETE: Not on your life. She's taking off her sweater. Which means she's walking right into it.

*(*SUZANNE *comes back on.)*

SUZANNE: *(Calling to* PETE*) Garcon! (Handing him her sweater)* Hold this for me, *s'il vous plait.*

PETE: *(Taking it; bowing, with his best prep-school French) Enchante, mademoiselle.*

SUZANNE: *(To* UMPIRE*)* Monsieur Tilden has invited me to play a regular match. The poor man seems almost desperate. *(She goes off)*

PETE: *(To* UMPIRE*)* Now you've got to look.

UMPIRE: No thank you.

PETE: I want a ringside seat. This is one for the books! *(He tosses the sweater on a chair, hurries off.)*

(Tennis sounds)

(Lights focus on the UMPIRE *who works on tournament planning, unwilling to watch the match.)*

(Then cheers and applause. TILDEN *comes on, arm around* PETE, *laughing.)*

TILDEN: Game's over.

PETE: You can say that again!

TILDEN: We slaughtered her, didn't we, Pete?

PETE: Six-love. She hardly got to deuce.

TILDEN: She wouldn't even consider a second set.

PETE: "Frailty, thy name is woman," right, Bill?

TILDEN: That's one way of putting it.

UMPIRE: Congratulations.

TILDEN: Will you be making a report of this?

UMPIRE: No.

TILDEN: I mean just for the record.

UMPIRE: No.

PETE: People will want to know.

UMPIRE: People will find out.

TILDEN: We drew quite a crowd.

PETE: I saw a guy taking pictures.

UMPIRE: He'll probably sell it to the newspapers.

TILDEN: I can see the headlines: "France Falls"...

PETE: Or how about "Weaker Sex Meets Waterloo"?

UMPIRE: Something like that.

TILDEN: *(Towelling himself off)* She had these strange
little jumps. Most of which are totally unnecessary.

(He imitates her. PETE imitates him.)

PETE: She should switch to ballet, right, Bill?

TILDEN: *(To UMPIRE)* Her game's not bad, Fred. It's just
wrong. Like the music of Debussy. Too many roulades,
very little underlying structure.

UMPIRE: You must feel very satisfied.

TILDEN: *(Gathering up his stuff)* I do...I feel... *(Stops as
SUZANNE comes on to retrieve her sweater)*

SUZANNE: *(Quietly, with dignity)* Merci, Monsieur.
You played very well indeed. *(She bows to him,
picks up her sweater, and and goes.)*

PETE: *(Watching her go; then to others)* Boo-hoo.
Right, Bill?

(Pause)

TILDEN: *(To UMPIRE)* How can I make it up?

UMPIRE: I'm not sure you can. *(Starts out)*

TILDEN: Wait, Freddy. Wait. Remember that girl
you said wanted to take lessons?

UMPIRE: Gloria Butler.

TILDEN: Right. Gloria. She reminds me of that song, "Angel Child."

PETE: *(Singing a bar or two)* "Angel child..."

UMPIRE: Do you want to beat her, too?

TILDEN: I want to give her lessons.

PETE: *(Stopping singing)* Are you serious, Bill?

TILDEN: Very much so.

UMPIRE: *(Going off)* She'll be delighted to hear that.

TILDEN: *(Calling after him)* For free, of course.

UMPIRE: I should hope so.

TILDEN: Spread the word. I'll give lessons to any woman who's willing to learn from a rotter like me.

PETE: How about *my* lessons, Bill?

TILDEN: I've already given you some.

PETE: I could use more. I'm thinking of staying over. My Dad wants me to make the Yale tennis team.

TILDEN: Good luck.

PETE: Gee whiz, Bill. We've still got a long way to go.

TILDEN: I think you and I have gone quite far enough.

(PETE walks out, hurt. TILDEN moves away.)

(SECOND ACTOR comes on, carrying a manuscript in a black binder. He now is an EDITOR at a publishing house.)

EDITOR: I'm confused, Bill.

TILDEN: *(As he puts on a jacket)* You confused, Harry? Never.

EDITOR: I'm your book editor. I do books. *(Indicating manuscript)* Here you've written a play.

TILDEN: Do you like it?

EDITOR: Bill, my friend, your books on tennis are exceptional. "The Art of Lawn Tennis" has sold beautifully. "Match Play and the Spin of the Ball." is already recognized as a classic.

TILDEN: What about my short stories?

EDITOR: People get a kick out of your titles, Bill.

TILDEN: I know it. "Mixed Troubles"... "Foot Fault." ... "Love Means Nothing" ... And they sell, too.

EDITOR: They do, Bill. To a limited market. Consisting primarily of adolescent male tennis players.

TILDEN: That's why I broadened my base with my novel.

EDITOR: You did indeed, Bill. Your novel appealed to older male tennis players.

TILDEN: It was about more than tennis, Harry.

EDITOR: Yes it was, Bill. It was about women. Good women and bad women. The good women stay home and cook. The bad women lure men away from tennis.

TILDEN: So what's the problem?

EDITOR: *(Indicating manuscript)* Why a play?

TILDEN: Why not?

EDITOR: Plays are tricky things, Bill. They require actors, names, stars.

TILDEN: I'm a name. I'll star in it myself.

EDITOR: Athletes don't go on stage.

TILDEN: Ty Cobb did. Johnny Weismuller is playing Tarzan in the movies. I'm just as famous. People will pay to see me.

EDITOR: Bill, my good friend, you have no acting experience.

TILDEN: I've been acting all my life.

EDITOR: You'll need a director, a producer, backers....

TILDEN: I'll do all that myself.

EDITOR: That's known as vanity, Bill.

TILDEN: What isn't vanity, in the end? I'm used to being my own man.

EDITOR: The theater isn't tennis, Bill.

TILDEN: Maybe it's better. You can control who wins and loses. You can control the audience.

EDITOR: Can you control the critics?

(The FIRST ACTOR *comes on as a* CRITIC, *in tweedy jacket and bow tie. He sits aside in a special light.)*

TILDEN: *(Settling at the change-over table, as if it were now his dressing table)* We'll see.

CRITIC: *(Reading from his note book)* "For an actor, Tilden is a pretty good tennis player."

EDITOR: *(Showing* TILDEN *a newspaper)* Bad reviews can hurt, Bill.

TILDEN: So I lost the first set.

CRITIC: "Mr Tilden keeps his amateur standing in this one"...

TILDEN: *(As he begins to make up at the table)* As I say in my books, the game itself is more important than the final score.

CRITIC: "Mr Tilden so rolls his eyes and writhes his lower jaw as to suggest that shortly before the birth of his dramatic ambitions, he was badly frightened by Alfred Lunt."

EDITOR: *(Indicating newspaper)* That was a low blow. He's comparing you to one of our best actors.

TILDEN: *(As if putting on make-up)* I take that as a compliment. In fact, I intend to perform in several plays that Lunt made famous. The part's the thing, and Lunt picked the good ones.

CRITIC: "The direction was deplorable, and Tilden himself pretty bad, but the audience seemed to find it agreeable to see Mr Tilden do anything imperfectly."

TILDEN: *(Putting the paper aside)* See? They like me. Love me, in fact. I feel it across the footlights.

EDITOR: I hear you now want to play Dracula.

TILDEN: Sure. You know why? Because then they'll love me even when I'm evil. I plan to try it out on the West Coast before bringing it into New York.

EDITOR: Good luck, Bill. At least with Dracula the critics can't accuse you of overacting.

(EDITOR goes to one side. TILDEN puts in fake fangs, tosses on a large black cape, twirling it as he steps onto the "stage".)

(Creepy music and fog)

(ACTRESS comes on as MISS EMERSON, the ingenue.)

TILDEN: Ah , Miss Emerson, what an enchanting creature you are! May I kiss your hand?

MISS EMERSON: Oh sir, oh sir, I do not know you.

TILDEN: I am Count Dracula, Madam.

MISS EMERSON: Oh my! I've heard of you, sir. The villagers say you are steeped in mystery.

TILDEN: Do I frighten you, my dear?

CRITIC: *(Again reading from his notes)* "Mr Tilden has memorized the other actor's parts, as well as his own. If you get bored with watching the others, you may always watch Tilden mouthing their lines."

MISS EMERSON: (*As* TILDEN *mouths her lines*) Frighten me? Oh sir, you do. But you fascinate me as well. There is a darkness in you, an ache, a deep, sad longing for the rich red juice of life which draws me to you. But I feel you are corrupt.

TILDEN: Corrupt? Ah no, Madam, I'm simply cold. May I touch my cold lips to your warm neck?

MISS EMERSON: (TILDEN *speaking along with her*) Oh sir, oh sir, oh sir

(TILDEN *kisses her, masking it with his cloak*)

(*Applause and lights. They take their bows as* TILDEN *again masks* MISS EMERSON *with his cloak.*)

CRITIC: (*Reading his review*) "Tilden poaches on his fellow actors' territory as thoroughly as he does on doubles partners'. But for all his extra efforts, it is doubtful that this production will move past Pasadena."

MISS EMERSON: (*Contemptuously, over her shoulder toward* TILDEN) Amateur!

(*She and the* CRITIC *go off.*)

(TILDEN *returns to his table to remove his "make-up".*)

EDITOR: Stick with your books on tennis, Bill.

TILDEN: Not on your life, Harry. Now I'm in California, I'm writing a movie. I plan to direct it and act in it myself, like my good friend Charles Chaplin. I'm calling it *Hands of Hope*, and it will be about keeping a firm grip—on life, not just on a tennis racquet.

EDITOR: (*As he goes*) One thing about you, Bill. You don't give up.

TILDEN: (*Calling after him*) Don't dare, Harry. Don't dare.

(FIRST ACTOR *returns as the* UMPIRE.)

UMPIRE: Bill: Rene Lacoste has challenged you to a special international match.

TILDEN: When?

UMPIRE: Next month, when he comes over. He wants to revenge the honor of Suzanne Lenglen.

TILDEN: I'm a little tired, Fred.

UMPIRE: You should be. Between tournaments you've been dashing up to New Hampshire to teach tennis to poor kids at some camp.

TILDEN: Sometimes I wonder what I'm trying to prove. My good friend Richard Halliburton is in the same bind. He became a celebrity by swimming the Bosphorus and crossing the Alps on an elephant. Now everyone thinks he should climb Mount Everest. And he hates the cold.

UMPIRE: You don't hate tennis, Bill.

TILDEN: I hate to lose. And I'm beginning to.
(He takes up his racket and goes off.)

(SECOND ACTOR and a YOUNG ACTOR come on as MIKE and JIMMY, father and son.)

MIKE: Tilden, Tilden, Tilden... For Chrissake, why do we have to see every match he plays?

JIMMY: Because this summer may be our last chance, Dad. All the great athletes are falling around him. Bobby Jones losing in golf, Dempsey losing to Tunney, Babe Ruth bowing out—the sportwriters say it's the twilight of the gods.

(They settle into the stands.)

UMPIRE: *(Through his megaphone)* Game, set, match for Mr Lacoste.

(More crowd sounds)

MIKE: When I was your age, I watched baseball.
I went to baseball games with *my* dad.

JIMMY: I like tennis.

MIKE: Tennis. It's always the same, tennis.

JIMMY: That's because you don't know the game, Dad.

UMPIRE: *(Through his megaphone)* Game, set, match for
Mr Morgan.

MIKE: I do know that Tilden just lost again.

JIMMY: But what masterful strokes!

MIKE: You like losers, go watch the Red Sox.

JIMMY: Lay off, Dad. Please.

MIKE: Ho hum. Sure you don't want to be at the flower
show?

UMPIRE: *(Calling out)* Game to Mr Doeg. He leads, five
games to four, in the third set.

*(*WOMAN *comes on as* ANDREA, *in a sexy outfit)*

ANDREA: *(To* MIKE*)* I've come to see the famous Bill
Tilden.

MIKE: *(Making a space for her)* Be my guest.

ANDREA: I assume he's the handsome one scampering
around in back.

MIKE: Handsome? That guy?

ANDREA: Very. And I hear they call him the Great
Gatsby of tennis.

MIKE: The Great who?

JIMMY: Gatsby, Dad. It's a book. *(To* ANDREA
The sports writers sometimes call him that.
Because he's a man of mystery.

MIKE: What is this? The ladies culture club.

ANDREA: Quiet, sir. I'm learning something. *(To* JIMMY*)*
Tell me, sonny: do the sports pages say there's a Daisy
Buchanan in the picture?

JIMMY: I never read that.

ANDREA: Or maybe there's a Mrs Tilden, waiting in the
wings.

JIMMY: They don't say.

MIKE: Hey, fellas. Save it for the gossip columns, O K?

ANDREA: *(To* JIMMY*)* I'll deal with him. *(To* MIKE*)*
I'm just sizing things up. I can never watch athletes
without imagining them in bed.

MIKE: Does that apply to bowling?

*(*TILDEN *comes on angrily, limping.)*

TILDEN: I can't continue. There's too much random
chatter in the stands.

UMPIRE: Bill ...

TILDEN: I've fallen down, I've hurt my knee, and you
people are chattering like magpies. I've always said that
a tennis star owes his public a good game. Well, you
owe *me* your undivided attention.

UMPIRE: Play tennis, Bill.

TILDEN: I'd be glad to. *(To stands)* As soon as somebody
around here realizes that I'm in an uphill battle and I'm
fighting for my goddam *life! (He goes off angrily.)*

ANDREA: *(To* MIKE*)* Uh-oh.

MIKE: What?

ANDREA: He's a fruit fly.

MIKE: No.

ANDREA: He's a flit. I could tell from that tantrum.

MIKE: Tilden?

ANDREA: *(Loud whisper to* JIMMY*)* There's your mystery, sonny! The man is a full-fledged fairy queen!

MIKE: Come on, lady. The guy may be weird, he may even be a little swish, but no pansy could ever be a world champion.

ANDREA: Mark my words. Us girls can tell.

UMPIRE: *(Calling out)* Service, Mr Doeg. He leads, eleven games to ten in the fifth set.

(More tennis sounds)

MIKE: *(To* ANDREA*)* Wanna get a drink?

ANDREA: Now?

MIKE: I'm not going to stand around watching some poof.

ANDREA: Let's go.

MIKE: *(Calling to* JIMMY*)* We'll be in the bar, Jim!

JIMMY: *(Crossing to them)* Dad! It's eleven to ten in the *fifth set!*

ANDREA: We've lost interest, sonny. For reasons which some day you'll understand.

MIKE: *(To* ANDREA*)* No wonder I don't dig this fruity game.

JIMMY: Dad!

MIKE: Come when it's over. I'll buy you a soda-pop.

ANDREA: *(Taking his arm)* Why oh why are the most attractive men in the world always a little peculiar?

MIKE: I'm the exception to that rule, baby.

ANDREA: Oh yes. I could tell that, too, immediately.

(They go off. JIMMY *remains.)*

UMPIRE: Game, set and match to Mr Doeg.

(Applause; TILDEN *comes on, exhausted)*

TILDEN: *(Angrily throwing down his racket)* I've played on grass all my life, but that was a cow pasture. How can a man possibly— *(He checks himself, remembering that he is supposed to shake the* UMPIRE'*s hand at the end of a match. He goes to shake it.)* Oh heavens! Listen to me. Not only have I lost the match, but now I'm becoming a poor sport! *(As if to the stands)* Learn how to lose, people. Lose cheerfully and generously. This is the first and greatest commandment. And the second is like unto it: it's always better to win.

UMPIRE: You can play him again this fall, Bill. In Paris.

TILDEN: Sorry, my friend. I'm turning pro.

UMPIRE: What? This from the man who has constantly sworn he'd never play for money?

TILDEN: Everyone plays for it now. Amateur tennis is "shamateur tennis" these days.

UMPIRE: Now Bill...

TILDEN: Admit it, Freddie. We're all being paid under the table. But even after all the perks and gifts and honoraria, I'm still dead broke.

UMPIRE: If you go pro, you'll be ostracized, Bill. You'll have to resign from the Lawn Tennis Association.

TILDEN: That won't break my heart.

UMPIRE: Yes, but you'll no longer be able to play at any club. Which means Wimbledon, and Longwood, and Forest Hills - they're clubs, too, Bill. They'll all shut their doors to any player who makes money from tennis.

TILDEN: Because they'll make less money themselves.

UMPIRE: You'll have to settle for one-night stands in local auditoriums on slippery surfaces with lousy locker rooms. In the theater they call it barn-storming.

TILDEN: At least the game will remain the same.

UMPIRE: Will it, Bill? A bunch of exhibition matches against second-rate opponents? With nothing to win at the end?

TILDEN: Except money, Fred.

UMPIRE: Money, money, money.

TILDEN: I have to live, Freddie. And I like to live well. Which means I need more than the hand-outs I get from you.

UMPIRE: Oh, Bill. It will be a come-down, all the way.

TILDEN: Who knows? Maybe I can make it a step up.

(UMPIRE *looks at him and leaves.*)

(*A moment as* TILDEN *rubs his ankle, towels off*)

(JIMMY, *who has been watching from one side, now approaches him.*)

JIMMY: Great game, Mr Tilden.

TILDEN: Gets tougher every time.

JIMMY: (*Crossing to him; taking out his program*) Could I have your autograph, sir?

(*He doesn't have a pencil.* TILDEN *produces one.*)

TILDEN: Oh sure. Why not? (*Signs*)

JIMMY: Say. How do you get to be a ball-boy, Mr Tilden?

TILDEN: Oh well. There are ball-boys. And ball-boys.

JIMMY: What does it take to be a good one?

TILDEN: A burning love of the game.

JIMMY: I've sure got that.

TILDEN: A passionate desire to learn more about it.

JIMMY: I've read all your books.

TILDEN: And it takes time, my friend. Now I'm going pro, I plan to bring my ball-boys with me. Which means time away from school. Time away from family.

JIMMY: I'd like that.

TILDEN: *(Sitting)* It will be a lonely life, on tour. No more carte blanche at the local country club. No more bridge games after dinner. No more guest rooms with fresh-cut flowers. *(To (*JIMMY*)* I suppose you don't care about these things.

JIMMY: Not really.

TILDEN: *(Indicating a nearby chair for* JIMMY *to sit)* There are compensations, too. For a ball-boy. For example, a player might warm up with a ball-boy as the crowd is coming in.

JIMMY: I'd love that.

TILDEN: And they might have dinner together afterwards. To go over the game. Oh, and do you play gin rummy?

JIMMY: I can learn.

TILDEN: Otherwise I might be playing lots of solitaire back at some gloomy downtown hotel. In order to unwind.

JIMMY: I'll play gin rummy with you, Mr Tilden.

TILDEN: *(Getting up)* And your name is?

JIMMY: Jim.

TILDEN: *(Tossing* JIMMY *his racket)* I'd like to take you on, Jimmy... *(Stopping)* Do you think your parents will let you go?

JIMMY: I'm not sure about that.

TILDEN: Tell them I'll be responsible. I'll be your father, and teacher, and friend. Will that do it?

JIMMY: No, but I'll go anyway, Bill.

(JIMMY *exits as* SECOND ACTOR *comes on as* MADDOX, *reading a document.*)

MADDOX: *(Reading aloud)* "I sincerely regret my actions and desire that the court permit me to prove that my recent behavior does not reflect my true nature and my better self...."

(TILDEN *returns, now in his camel hair coat.*)

TILDEN: *(Reading over his shoulder)* "...I have learned my lesson and will never forget it." *(To* MADDOX*)* How does that sound, Richard? Will it keep me out of the clink?

MADDOX: If the judge buys it.

TILDEN: The probation officer wrote a letter on my behalf. He said jail would do me more harm than good.

MADDOX: It damn well might.

TILDEN: And the psychiatrist wrote, too. He thinks they should view me as someone who's mentally ill.

MADDOX: He recommends electric shock treatments.

TILDEN: Good God, I hope I'm not *that* bad.

MADDOX: How bad are you, Bill?

TILDEN: What do you mean?

MADDOX: The ball boys you bring along on your tours. The sports columns have mentioned them.

TILDEN: Ball boys are a part of the game.

MADDOX: We should have pleaded not guilty, Bill.

TILDEN: I couldn't do that.

MADDOX: Christ Bill, sometimes I think you want to be caught.

TILDEN: The psychiatrist said that, too.

MADDOX: Careening down Sunset Boulevard in an open convertible on a Saturday night, with some unlicensed kid at the wheel. Signing a full confession, and then rejecting legal advice.

(UMPIRE *comes on as* JUDGE. YOUNG ACTOR *comes on as a* COP, *stands to one side*)

TILDEN: What's your advice now?

MADDOX: Tell the truth.

TILDEN: The truth being...?

MADDOX: That you've got a major problem and you need major psychiatric help. Tell the judge that, and you've got half a chance. The truth shall set thee free.

JUDGE: (*Banging his gavel*) Order in the court... You may sit down, counsel.

(MADDOX *sits.*)

JUDGE: Mr Tilden, would you approach the bench, please...

(TILDEN *approaches the* JUDGE)

I've read your written statement, Mr Tilden, and now I must ask you a few questions.

TILDEN: Certainly, your honor.

JUDGE: How long have you been engaged in athletics?

TILDEN: I've played tennis all my life, sir.

JUDGE: All your life?

TILDEN: (*After a glance at* MADDOX) I say that because my life before tennis was no life at all.

JUDGE: Setting aside the harm you might do to others, Mr Tilden, did you ever give any thought to the harm you could do to yourself, if you were caught doing what you've done?

TILDEN: No sir. I don't think I thought of that.

JUDGE: Because you never thought you'd be caught?

TILDEN: Because I've never done it before.

(MADDOX *coughs noisily.*)

JUDGE: Never?

TILDEN: *(After glancing at* MADDOX*)* Oh, once, as a young boy, I was very stupid ...

JUDGE: But that's it?

TILDEN: That's it, sir.

(MADDOX *groans.*)

JUDGE: You said something, Mr Maddox?

MADDOX: No, but I wanted to.

(TILDEN *starts to joins* MADDOX.*)

JUDGE: Please remain standing, Mr Tilden.

TILDEN: Yes sir.

JUDGE: May I ask you another personal question?

TILDEN: Of course, your honor.

JUDGE: Have you ever had relations with women?

MADDOX: *(Jumping up)* I object, your honor...

TILDEN: *(To* MADDOX*)* No, Richard. That's all right. *(To* JUDGE*)* Relations with women. Yes sir. I have. *(Pause)* Once. When I was in the Army. With a prostitute. After having consumed a considerable amount of alcohol.

JUDGE: And?

TILDEN: It was so repulsive to me that I was sick to my stomach.

JUDGE: So you've had no further experiences with women?

TILDEN: No sir. No women since. No alcohol, either, I hasten to add.

JUDGE: And you say no boys?

(MADDOX *leans forward.*)

TILDEN: No, sir. Except for this incident, sir.

MADDOX: May I speak to my client, you honor?

JUDGE: It's too late for that, Mr Maddox ... I'll ask you to remain standing while you are sentenced, Mr Tilden. Would you join us, Mr Maddox?

(MADDOX *gets up and stands by* TILDEN.)

JUDGE: William Tatem Tilden the Second: the court at this time sentences you to the county jail for a period of one year.

TILDEN: Jail? *(His knees buckle; he falls to the floor.)*

JUDGE: Upon release, you will place yourself under the care of a competent psychiatrist.

MADDOX: If the court please ...

JUDGE: I am not finished, Mr Maddox ... *(To* TILDEN*)* Also upon release, you will strive at all times to be a law-abiding citizen, Mr Tilden. You are not to be found alone in the company of any juvenile, of either sex.

MADDOX: May I propose ...

JUDGE: I am still not finished, Mr Maddox ... *(To* TILDEN*)* And I hope, Mr Tilden, this will serve as an object lesson to those parents who are unconcerned about the associations of their youngsters. There is too much of this going on here in Los Angeles and

elsewhere, and it's time it stopped! *(To* COP*)* Put the
sentence into effect immediately, *(He goes.)*

MADDOX: *(Low to* TILDEN*)* All he wanted was the truth.

COP: *(Holding out handcuffs)* Put your hands out, pal...
(Handcuffs TILDEN*)*

MADDOX: The truth, Bill! Why didn't you tell it?

COP: *(Leading* TILDEN *off)* Make tracks, buddy.

MADDOX: Bill! Why didn't you?

TILDEN: *(Stopping)* Admit something like that? With
those reporters sitting there, writing things down?
I am still a gentleman, Richard! At least in public!

(He goes off, supported by the COP.*)*

*(Broody Forties music. Shower sounds. The sense of a locker
room.* MADDOX *takes off his jacket, puts on dark glasses,
becomes* BENNY, *the manager of Tilden Tennis Tours Inc.*
TILDEN *comes out, partially dressed, toweling his hair as if
from a shower,* MADDOX *tosses him a towel. Ball boys comb
their hair, get dressed, go off. One remains, off to one side)*

BENNY: How come you never take a shower with the
other players?

TILDEN: What?

BENNY: You always wait and shower alone.

TILDEN: Benny, you're my manager on this tour, not my
psychiatrist. It's none of your business if I take a shower
or don't.

BENNY: It's everybody's business when you don't.

TILDEN: I'm a private person, Benny. I don't like
displaying my body in front of others. Never have.
Never will. It's vulgar and exhibitionist. I am a tennis
player, not a naked man. Now. How'd we do tonight?

BENNY: We'd do better if you let one of the other players else win occasionally. It would add a little suspense.

TILDEN: I don't throw matches, Benny.

BENNY: They do it in boxing.

TILDEN: Not in tennis, my friend. I will give points, I will give games, I will play to the crowd all along the way, but I will not throw a match, Benny. I'm still amateur enough to want to win fairly and squarely in the end. *(Puts on jacket)*

BENNY: Let's talk, Bill. I'll buy you dinner.

TILDEN: Thanks, but I'm grabbing a bite with Fritzie. *(Indicating BALL BOY, waiting to one side)*

BENNY: That's why we should talk. The other players are complaining.

TILDEN: That I have dinner with a ball-boy?

BENNY: They don't like how it looks.

(TILDEN tosses an overnight bag to FRITZIE, who then leaves.)

TILDEN: I'm teaching him tennis.

BENNY: At night?

TILDEN: Whenever I can.

BENNY: Last year it was Sandy.

TILDEN: And now Sandy is rated seventeenth among the Juniors.

BENNY: You see too much of them, Bill.

TILDEN: Hey look: when the match is over, you guys go kick up your heels with your wives or girl-friends. Why can't I have a quiet dinner with Fritzie?

BENNY: And spend the night with him?

TILDEN: Only if there are twin beds.

BENNY: Bill...

TILDEN: I sleep alone, Ben. Always have. Always will.
I don't even know what it's like to sleep the whole night
through with someone else.

BENNY: What about the fans, Bill? We're bringing in a
broader crowd now.

TILDEN: Thanks to me.

BENNY: Yeah well, folks are still a little dicey about
guys prancing around in shorts, saying "deuce" and
"love".

TILDEN: That's why I still wear long pants.

BENNY: Bill.

TILDEN: O K. "Love" is bad, I admit. I don't like "love."
I'm looking for a substitute for "love."

BENNY: Find a substitute for Fritzie.

TILDEN: Fritzie's eighteen. He a grown man.

BENNY: Date a woman occasionally. Get your picture
taken with her. Please.

TILDEN: Oh for God's sake, Benny! In Germany, several
players took their boys with them. People accept these
things in Germany.

BENNY: Not lately, they don't. That's why Fritzie can't
go back.

TILDEN: O K. Greece, then. Classical Greece. If you were
a teacher in ancient Greece, your relations with your
student were expected to be...well, exceptional.

BENNY: We're not Ancient Greece, Bill.

TILDEN: Maybe we should be. I mean, what's wrong
with relationships like that? Just because a man doesn't

generate children physically, why can't he still have
sons? Why can't we create them out of what we do?
And pass on to them what we know? And make them
truer, better offspring than the ones who are born from
some gross tussle in bed with a demanding female.
Read Plato, Benny.

BENNY: I'll rush to the library. Meanwhile, could you at
least be more discreet?

TILDEN: Meaning what?

BENNY: Don't rally with Fritzie in front of the crowd
before every goddam match. Don't eat with him in
restaurants. And get separate rooms. Please.

TILDEN: Ben, one quick question: how much money
have I personally netted in the seven years since I
turned pro?

BENNY: Approximately half a million.

TILDEN: And how much money have the others made?

BENNY: Not as much.

TILDEN: They'd make nothing, Benny, without me.
Nothing. I'm the guy people pay to see. You might
remind them of that. And after you've done that, please
ask Fritzie to meet me at Steve's Steak House—no!
Change that to the Parthenon Palace, for some Greek
cuisine. As for what happens afterwards, that's my
business, Benny. And Fritzie's. Period. (*Goes off*)

(*Tennis sounds. The* UMPIRE *comes on. He now uses a
microphone rather than a megaphone.*)

UMPIRE: Ladies and gentlemen: the final match of the
evening! The legendary Big Bill Tilden will now play
one set only against the undisputed professional tennis
champion of the world: Mr Don Budge!

(*Sounds of larger audience response now, as if we were in a
large stadium*)

(Lights isolate WOMAN *and* YOUNG ACTOR *downstage, simulating a high area of the stands. They are* MRS ANDERSON *and her son* ARTHUR, *who has binoculars)*

MRS ANDERSON: *(Settling into her seat)* Mercy! I've never seen such a crowd.

ARTHUR: That's because Big Bill Tilden is still a major draw. *(Handing his mother the binoculars)* He's in the left hand court, Mom. Here. Take a look.

MRS ANDERSON: *(Focusing the binoculars, looking)* He's an attractive man, I'll say that.

ARTHUR: And a great tennis player.

MRS ANDERSON: Why is he so interested in you?

ARTHUR: Because he saw me play. And likes my game.

UMPIRE: *(On microphone)* Mr Tilden will now serve.

ARTHUR: That's what he calls his cannon-ball serve.

MRS ANDERSON: Heavens. I could hardly see the ball.

ARTHUR: It used to be the most powerful serve in the world.

MRS ANDERSON: And he's teaching you to do that?

ARTHUR: He's teaching me everything. For free. Whenever he's not on tour.

UMPIRE: *(On microphone)* Advantage, Mr Budge.

(Crowd noises)

UMPIRE: Quiet, please.

MRS ANDERSON: And now he wants to stay with us?

ARTHUR: It was my idea, Mom. I told him about our extra room.

MRS ANDERSON: We're not running a boarding house, Arthur. Your father may have left us cold, but I have not yet sunk to that.

ARTHUR: We sure could use the rent.

MRS ANDERSON: And I suppose you could use another father.

ARTHUR: I could use a better serve, that I know.

UMPIRE: Game to Mr Budge

(More tennis sounds; they watch.)

MRS ANDERSON: I'm just not sure I want to bring a strange man into our home.

ARTHUR: He's not strange, Mother.

MRS ANDERSON: Mrs Wilson down the street says there are rumors about him.

ARTHUR: What rumors?

MRS ANDERSON: Well, that he's a bachelor...

ARTHUR: Yes? And?

MRS ANDERSON: ...and he has all these ball-boys running around...

ARTHUR: They go with the game, Mother.

MRS ANDERSON: Oh they do, do they? And what kind of game do they go with? I do know that with your father gone, I have to be aware of these things.

ARTHUR: I swear, Mother. He's never made a move on me.

MRS ANDERSON: What if he does?

ARTHUR: I'll tell him to knock it off immediately.

MRS ANDERSON: You've grown up very fast, Arthur.

ARTHUR: I've had to, Mom.

MRS ANDERSON: *(Taking the binoculars, looking through them again)* I must say, even from up here, you can't help but watch him.

ARTHUR: Once you've seen him , it's hard to watch anyone else.

MRS ANDERSON: Mrs Wilson said he comes from a fine Philadelphia family.

ARTHUR: Social register all the way ...

MRS ANDERSON: I don't know.... Taking in a boarder...

ARTHUR: A guest. An occasional houseguest. He'll be off on tour, most of the time.

UMPIRE: *(On microphone)* Out! The shot was called out!

(Crowd response. TILDEN *comes on hurriedly, sweaty from the game, carrying his racket.)*

TILDEN: *(To* UMPIRE*)* Who the hell is that linesman?

UMPIRE: He's the local hard court champion, Bill.

TILDEN: Get rid of him.

MRS ANDERSON: *(Looking through binoculars)* Now what's happening?

(Boos from the crowd)

UMPIRE: He's been calling them in your favor, Bill.

TILDEN: That's why he should go. He's blind as a bat. Throw him out of the game.

ARTHUR: *(To* MRS ANDERSON*)* Tilden doesn't like the linesman.

MRS ANDERSON: What if he doesn't like *me*?

ARTHUR: He's bound to, Mother. Everyone else does.

MRS ANDERSON: Oh pooh.

(Crowd sounds: "Boo, Tilden, Boo Tilden")

UMPIRE: That linesman is a crowd favorite around here, Bill.

(More booing)

TILDEN: Give me that microphone, please. *(He climbs up on the* UMPIRE'*s chair, takes the microphone, speaks as if to the entire stadium.)* Ladies and gentlemen...I hope you will allow a man to defend himself before you condemn him!

(Crowd quiets down.)

TILDEN: It is you, not I, who suffer the most from these bad calls. You have paid good money to watch me put up a match against Mr Don Budge. If I am disturbed by bad calls, I cannot play my best. And if you boo me, you only make it worse. If you want the most for your money, please hold off while I try to take on, fairly and squarely, Mr Budge, who is now undoubtedly the best player in the world. *(Hands the microphone back to the* UMPIRE*)*

MRS ANDERSON: At least he's a man of principle.

ARTHUR: That's it, Mother. You've got his number.

TILDEN: *(To* UMPIRE*)* Now tell your crowd favorite to get lost. *(He goes off to resume the game)*

ARTHUR: So you'll ask him?

MRS ANDERSON: I suppose we could ask him to tea.

UMPIRE: Game. Set. Match for Mr Budge.

(Cheering and applause)

*(*UMPIRE *goes off.)*

ARTHUR: And I'll show him the room.

MRS ANDERSON: But what if he asks for a cocktail? After your father, I refuse to have liquor in the house.

ARTHUR: Tilden doesn't drink, Mother.

MRS ANDERSON: What? A man who doesn't drink? Really?...

(They go off.)

(JUDGE *comes on in a special light*)

JUDGE: *(To audience; reading a document)* ... It has come to my attention that for a period of time prior to his incarceration Mr Tilden considered his place of residence to be the home of a Mrs William Anderson and son in Greater Los Angeles. Now that he is being discharged from the penitentiary, therefore, he will still be permitted to return there provided that he associate with younger persons only when they are accompanied by an adult at all times.

(JUDGE *goes off as DMRS ANDERSON throws a tablecloth over a table.* ARTHUR *comes on with a vase of flowers.*)

MRS ANDERSON: We'll simply pretend he's coming back from another one of those tennis tours.

ARTHUR: Right.

MRS ANDERSON: Everyone makes mistakes in this world, Arthur. Our job is to forgive and forget.

ARTHUR: I'm with you on that.

MRS ANDERSON: Did you clean up his room?

ARTHUR: I even polished his trophies.

MRS ANDERSON: There are so many. I had to put some of them in the attic.

ARTHUR: He won't have much money now, Mom. I don't think you should ask for rent.

MRS ANDERSON: I never did. He left it anyway. There it would be, always in an envelope, tucked under my door.

ARTHUR: He hates what he calls "a vulgar exchange of money."

MRS ANDERSON: That's because he's a gentleman, Arthur. A gentleman to the core. Which is why he deserves our best attentions.

ARTHUR: *(Looking out)* Here's his cab....

MRS ANDERSON: *(Primping in front of the mirror)* I'm suddenly terribly nervous. Do you know, I used to feel the same way when your father came home after one of his nights on the town.

ARTHUR: Sssshh.

*(*TILDEN *comes in, in his old camel hair coat, carrying a battered suitcase.)*

TILDEN: Howdy, howdy, howdy.

MRS ANDERSON: Welcome home, Bill. *(A polite kiss on his cheek)*

TILDEN: *(Looking around)* Home... What a wonderful word, "home". Do you know something? While I was away, I realized that this is the only real home I've ever had.

MRS ANDERSON: Oh no, you silly-billy. What about your relatives in Philadelphia?

TILDEN: They don't know me. Never did. But here, with you, I feel part of a real family. Marrian, you're my wife—in a manner of speaking. And Arthur, you're my son. *(A manly handshake)*

ARTHUR: I wish that would make me a better tennis player.

TILDEN: It will, it will, I'll see to that.

MRS ANDERSON: Guess what, Bill? I broke down and bought a bottle of champagne.

TILDEN: Not for me. But you should indulge, Marrian.

MRS ANDERSON: I thought maybe now that you're out of...

TILDEN: ...prison? Let me tell you something about prison, dear friends. Remember what I always say about playing to win, Arthur? Rather than just playing not to lose?

ARTHUR: Sure do, Bill.

TILDEN: Well sir, in jail, I played to win! I seized the hour. Manual labor is good, you know. It purifies the soul. So I worked. I worked hard. And in my free time, I wrote my autobiography. I put in my philosophy of life. I wrote that life is like a spring day, cloudy and sunny both. All right, maybe I am currently under a cloud, but I know the sun shines somewhere. I can glimpse a beam tinting the gloom and I take hope. That's what I wrote, almost word for word.

MRS ANDERSON: "Hope is the thing with feathers, that perches in the soul".

TILDEN: Emily Dickinson, right, Marrian?

MRS ANDERSON: Yes, yes...

TILDEN: Oh, and hey, while I was there, I also wrote a play, called *New Shoes*. *New Shoes*. Because I'm a new man now. And guess what? Judge Scott must have heard how well I was doing. That's why he gave me early release. You see? So in the end I've won my match, Arthur. Maybe not six-love, but I've still won.

ARTHUR: That's great, Bill.

TILDEN: Of course you may not want me to stay with you now. You have every right to kick me out.

MRS ANDERSON: Don't talk nonsense, Bill.

TILDEN: I'm still on probation, you know. They want me to have psychiatric care. And I'm not supposed to be alone with young people—of either sex. That means you, Arthur. (*A bow to* MRS ANDERSON) And of course you, too, Marrian.

MRS ANDERSON: (*Flattered*) Oh Bill.

ARTHUR: You're always welcome here, Bill.

MRS ANDERSON: It wouldn't be the same without you.

TILDEN: I knew you'd say that. Because you know me.
You know all about me. And I'm still welcome here.
Well, I want you both to know that I wrote Judge Scott
that what happened...will never happen again. I gave
him my word. As a gentleman. And as a sportsman.

ARTHUR: Everyone makes mistakes. Right, Mother?

MRS ANDERSON: That's exactly it.

TILDEN: *(Embracing her)* I can't tell you how I appreciate
that! *(Starts to embrace* ARTHUR, *then settles for shaking
hands)* I'm not a sentimental man, but I feel very, very
touched.

MRS ANDERSON: Let's have dinner, Bill... Arthur, take
Bill's coat.

ARTHUR: Food's on the stove.

*(*ARTHUR *and* MRS ANDERSON *go off.* TILDEN *remains.
The* JUDGE, *returns, with a stack of legal documents.
We are in his chambers now.)*

JUDGE: *(Looking through documents)* When did I let you
out of jail, Mr Tilden?

TILDEN: August, 1947, your honor.

JUDGE: That's hardly more than a year ago.

TILDEN: Yes sir.

JUDGE: And here you are, back again.

TILDEN: This time I was totally set up, sir.

JUDGE: Mr Tilden, I don't normally ask for private
meetings with persons accused of a crime, but I
thought we knew each other. We've met and we've
corresponded over similar circumstances.

TILDEN: Not similar at all, your honor! As you know, I am somewhat of a celebrity in Los Angeles, and there are people here who want to bring me down.

JUDGE: I see.

TILDEN: You know this town, sir.

JUDGE: I know this town very well. I'm not sure I know you.

TILDEN: I have a good alibi, Judge Scott, up and down the line.

JUDGE: Oh you do, do you?

TILDEN: Absolutely, sir. I can account for where I was all day long. First, I had a dentist appointment, then I got the car greased, then I had lunch with an old friend, then—

JUDGE: *(Indicating the documents)* I've read all the depositions, Mr Tilden. They don't account for where you were between eight and nine in the morning.

TILDEN: I believe I stated that I was delivering young Arthur Anderson to Hollywood High.

JUDGE: *(Indicating document)* Young Anderson claims here he didn't see you until later that day.

TILDEN: He's changed his mind on that, sir.

JUDGE: *(Ironically)* Oh yes. That's right. *(Looks at another document)* Here he modifies his recollection after a conversation with his mother.

TILDEN: Sir—

JUDGE: Mr Tilden, even if you were with young Arthur between eight and nine in the morning, you'd still be in trouble. Under the terms of your probation, you're not supposed to be alone with any juvenile under any circumstances.

TILDEN: I don't consider Arthur Anderson "any juvenile", sir.

JUDGE: Oh you don't.

TILDEN: No, sir. I consider him my son. I've virtually adopted him. I'm teaching him everything I know, and some day he will be a great tennis player.

JUDGE: *(Vehemently)* Let's stop playing games now, Mr Tilden! This is not tennis! *(Taking a document out of his folder)* Last Tuesday, between eight and nine in the morning you picked up a young hitch-hiker on Wilshire Boulevard, and according to his statement, you placed your right hand repeatedly on his privates, despite his attempts to remove it. *(Reading)* Question, addressed to the boy: "Did the accused say anything during this time?" The boy: "He kept saying his hand was cold." *(Looking up)* Subsequently, when the boy made his complaint to the police, he accurately described your automobile, including the tennis rackets in the back seat and the broken hood ornament. He even remembered your license number. It's a watertight case, Mr Tilden. Now let's have no more talk about set-ups and alibis and people wanting to bring you down.

TILDEN: Your honor, may I ask you something?

JUDGE: Go ahead.

TILDEN: If this had been one of those young girls in shorts and halters who wave at the cars along La Cienega Boulevard, would I be in the same difficulty?

JUDGE: If she were a minor...

TILDEN: Oh Lord, what's a minor, Judge Scott? I can tell you that these boys know more about life at sixteen than I ever will!

JUDGE: I doubt that, Mr Tilden.

TILDEN: Besides, what harm did I do? The first one seduced *me*. And the second...

JUDGE: ...asked you to remove your hand.

TILDEN: Which I did.

JUDGE: Finally.

TILDEN: Your honor, never, *never* in my life, have I... imposed myself on another human being. Even with that prostitute long ago, I didn't...complete the.... All I have done, sir, all I have ever done in that regard is...touch occasionally...feel occasionally...mutually engage in...things that boys do, many boys do...when they're young.

JUDGE: You're not a boy any more, Mr Tilden.

TILDEN: My psychiatrist says I am.

JUDGE: I'm not your psychiatrist, sir.

TILDEN: Do you really think I've ruined these boys' lives?

JUDGE: I think you've ruined your own. You are a criminal, sir!

TILDEN: I am *not* a criminal! I am a tennis player. What's more...I feel awkward saying this—but I consider myself an artist, an artist of the game. Other people have said so, too. Sportswriters, tennis players, the great opera star Mary Garden have all told me the same thing. I am an artist! I have to create! And now that I'm getting too old to create my own game, I have to create it in others. I have to pass on what I know.

JUDGE: To the young?

TILDEN: To whomever wants to learn.

JUDGE: *(Taking out a document)*; reading from it) Do you remember writing this, Mr Tilden? *(Reading)* "The first law of tennis is that every player must be a good sportsman and inherently a gentleman."

TILDEN: That's from my book, *The Art of Lawn Tennis.*

JUDGE: And do you still believe in that law?

TILDEN: Yes I do. Though I have to say that once you turn pro, once the game becomes about money, it's hard to remain a gentleman.

JUDGE: And what is a "sportsman", Mr Tilden.

TILDEN: Someone who plays by the rules.

JUDGE: Someone who keeps his word?

TILDEN: Absolutely.

JUDGE: You wrote me a letter from prison, promising to refrain when you got out. You gave me your word as a sportsman, do you remember?

(Pause)

TILDEN: Well, sir...

JUDGE: You broke your word, Mr Tilden.

(Another pause)

TILDEN: Yes, but you see ...

JUDGE: You are not a sportsman, Mr Tilden. You were once a great athlete. You may still be an excellent teacher. You are possibly an artist. But you are no longer a sportsman nor a gentleman. You are a pederast. Mr Tilden!

TILDEN: *(Breaking down)* I can't help myself, sir.

JUDGE: Because your hand gets cold?

TILDEN: *(Weeping)* Because I get cold, all over. *(Pause)*

JUDGE: Have you ever loved anyone, Mr Tilden?

TILDEN: Yes, I have. I loved my mother very much. And she died. I loved my father. And he died soon after. And my dear brother—he was a true friend. And he died, too, the following year.

JUDGE: And you've loved no one else?

TILDEN: I love tennis.

(*Pause*)

JUDGE: What am I going to do with you, Mr Tilden?

TILDEN: I don't know, I don't know, I don't know.

JUDGE: What about your sessions with the psychiatrist?

TILDEN: They didn't help.

JUDGE: What if you went for more?

TILDEN: Sir, I know my own nature. In the end, I'm back to little Junie Tilden, the sissy, fooling around behind the barn.

JUDGE: Oh dear Lord.

TILDEN: Maybe you should lock me up forever.

JUDGE: No, sir. I'll send you back to jail for violating your probation, and let your punishment for this latest episode run simultaneously. And this time I'll ask that you be assigned to road service up north.. Maybe the snow and frigid air will help. You may get cold, Mr Tilden, but perhaps clearing our mountain highways will keep you warm.

TILDEN: Why are you going easy on me, sir?

JUDGE: Because the world will punish you more than the law ever could.

TILDEN: Oh I've been booed before.

JUDGE: This time they'll do worse than boo you, Mr Tilden. They'll ignore you.

(JUDGE goes. TILDEN remains)

(We hear sentimental Fifties Christmas music.)

(ARTHUR comes on, carrying a tennis racket and a suitcase.)

ARTHUR: We heard they're letting you out early for Christmas, Bill.

TILDEN: The court won't allow me to go home with you this time. Arthur.

ARTHUR: I know. *(Handing him the racket)* But they allowed me to give you this.

TILDEN: My best Bancroft! My Tilden-winner! *(Kisses it)* Thank you, Arthur.

ARTHUR: Will you play when you get out?

TILDEN: Can't do anything else. *(He flourishes it.)*

ARTHUR: You're still the best tennis player in the world, Bill.

TILDEN: For one set, maybe. With the sun behind me.

(MRS ANDERSON comes on, calling to him, as ARTHUR goes.)

MRS ANDERSON: Bill! ...Bill Tilden!...

TILDEN: Well, look who's here. *(He bows.)* The lovely Maid Marrian ....

MRS ANDERSON: *(Again flattered)* Oh Bill...I knew I'd find you teaching tennis.

TILDEN: Asphalt-surface. Riddled with pot holes. But it's a public court so they can't prevent me.

MRS ANDERSON: Arthur and I have found you a wonderful place to stay, Bill.

TILDEN: I've got a place, thanks.

MRS ANDERSON: No, but this is lovely and light, Bill. Do you remember Gloria Butler?

TILDEN: Gloria? Angel child? She was my first female tennis student.

MRS ANDERSON: You'll be living right above her.

TILDEN: So she can keep an eye on me?

MRS ANDERSON: So we can all see more of you, Bill.

TILDEN: Ganging up on me, eh?

MRS ANDERSON: We don't want to lose you. Now come and take a look.

(*They start off together as* SECOND ACTOR *comes on as* MADDOX.)

MADDOX: You wanted to see me, Bill?

TILDEN: (*Turning toward him , handing him a pen*) I bought you a present, Richard.

MADDOX: Many thanks... A fountain pen.

TILDEN: A small token, compared to what I owe you.

MADDOX: Why a pen, Bill?

TILDEN: So you can write my story. You know it better than most.

MADDOX: You're the writer, Bill.

TILDEN: But you're the lawyer. You could make my case. You could say...you could say that if only I had lived in a more accommodating society, I might have met someone...someone I could have loved...someone with whom I could have shared my life, without fear or shame.

MADDOX: And if you had, you might never have become a great champion, Bill.

TILDEN: You mean I lose either way?

MADDOX: That's what they call tragedy, Bill.

TILDEN: Then why not write that?

(He puts his suitcase on the table, begins to pack it as MADDOX *goes off.)*

*(*MRS ANDERSON *comes on again.)*

MRS ANDERSON: Knock, knock! It's your old landlady again!

TILDEN: My *former* landlady, you mean.. Nothing old about you, Marrian.

MRS ANDERSON: *(Flattered once again)* Oh Bill. *(Coming in)* I've got your money.

TILDEN: Good, good.

MRS ANDERSON: Where are you going, if I may ask?

TILDEN: Cleveland, Ohio. A few old-timers have asked me to play in the U S Professional Championships at Lakeland Park.

MRS ANDERSON: That's wonderful! Why didn't you tell us?

TILDEN: Didn't dare. These things can get canceled at the last minute, once folks hear I'm involved. Remember last year at the Beverly Hills Hotel?

MRS ANDERSON: I won't go near that place now. And I've told all my friends not to.

TILDEN: Well, this tournament seems set, and I need the cash to get there. Which is why I asked you to sell my trophies. I'm still too embarrassed to do it myself.

MRS ANDERSON: *(Putting the money down on the table)* It's not much this time, Bill. Only forty-five dollars.

TILDEN: For each?

MRS ANDERSON: For all .

TILDEN: *(Looking at money)* The silver alone is worth twice that.

MRS ANDERSON: Which is exactly what I told them.

TILDEN: *(Picks up the money, pockets it)* Yes well, I'll still give the folks in Cleveland their money's worth.

MRS ANDERSON: I'm sure you will, Bill. When do you leave?

TILDEN: The eleven o'clock train.

MRS ANDERSON: *(Starting out)* Tonight? Then I'll dash home and cook you a going-away dinner. Arthur can take you to the station afterwards.

TILDEN: Fine and dandy.

MRS ANDERSON: *(Stopping)* You look tired, Bill.

TILDEN: Oh I've caught a little cold.

MRS ANDERSON: Now that's because—

TILDEN: I know, I know. Shouldn't be teaching tennis in this cold weather. I think I'll go lie down for a minute.

(They go off either way. Organ music: Now the Day is Over. *MADDOX comes on hurriedly in an overcoat, then stops as* MRS ANDERSON *comes on, wearing a black hat or shawl.)*

MADDOX: I just got back. Is the service over?

MRS ANDERSON: It was very short.

MADDOX: How did it happen? The papers didn't say.

MRS ANDERSON: He was getting ready for a tournament in Cleveland. Arthur found him lying on his bed with his tennis rackets beside him. The coroner said it was just a case of a chap sixty years old who outlived his heart.

MADDOX: Typical Tilden. Rackets at the ready. Even at the end.

(ARTHUR comes on)

ARTHUR: There should have been more people.

MADDOX: I see Pancho Segura came.

MRS ANDERSON: And a group of other tennis players.

ARTHUR: *(Looking off)* Pretty small group.

MRS ANDERSON: Gloria specially bought a black dress.

ARTHUR: Angel child.

MRS ANDERSON: Oh, and Joseph Cotton was there, with his wife. *(To MADDOX)* He insisted that Bill be buried in his old white V-neck sweater.

ARTHUR: There should have been a huge crowd.

MRS ANDERSON: Some man said he was from Life magazine.

MADDOX: Maybe he'll write an article, Arthur.

ARTHUR: Yeah, but where was the U S Lawn Tennis Association? They didn't even send a wreath!

MRS ANDERSON: Make the best of it, dear.

ARTHUR: Goddammit, he deserves a better send off!

(Suddenly bright music from the Twenties, romantic lighting, sounds of a crowd cheering)

(The UMPIRE comes out with his megaphone)

UMPIRE: Game, set, and match to Mr Big Bill Tilden!

(Everyone gathers around. TILDEN bounces on, looking young and energetic. He wears his usual white sweater and pants and carries his wooden tennis racket. ARTHUR hands the UMPIRE a large silver cup, with a statuette of a serving tennis player on top)

UMPIRE: *(Continuing as he reads from the trophy)* For William Tatem Tilden, the Second...athlete, writer, actor, teacher, and above all, father of the game of tennis, who transformed it from a casual diversion of the wealthy few into a proud and passionate contest among his many children all over the world.

(He gives TILDEN *the trophy, shaking his hand.)*

UMPIRE: Congratulations, Bill.

TILDEN: *(Beaming proudly, holding his racket and the trophy)* Thank you. Thank you very much.

(Applause. Music. The others move out of the light, leaving TILDEN *standing alone in the light, nodding, bowing, waving as the light fades on him.)*

END OF PLAY